Pebble® Plus

Exploring the Galaxy

# The Sun

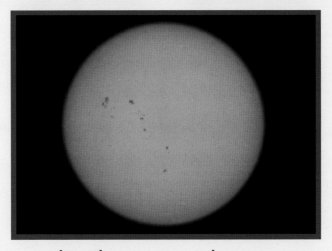

by Thomas K. Adamson

**Consulting Editor:** Gail Saunders-Smith, PhD

**Consultant:** Roger D. Launius, PhD
Chair, Division of Space History
National Air and Space Museum
Smithsonian Institution, Washington, D.C.

Capstone
press®

Mankato, Minnesota

Pebble Plus is published by Capstone Press,
151 Good Counsel Drive, P.O. Box 669, Mankato, Minnesota 56002.
www.capstonepub.com

*Library of Congress Cataloging-in-Publication Data*
Adamson, Thomas K., 1970–
    The Sun / by Thomas K. Adamson.
    p. cm.—(Pebble plus. Exploring the galaxy)
    Includes bibliographical references and index.
    ISBN 978-0-7368-6757-3 (hardcover)
    ISBN 978-1-4296-6290-1 (softcover)
    1. Sun—Juvenile literature. I. Title. II. Series.
QB521.5.A345 2007
523.7—dc22                                                                    2006023558

Summary: Simple text and photographs describe the Sun.

**Editorial Credits**
Katy Kudela, editor; Kia Adams, set designer; Mary Bode, book designer and illustrator; Jo Miller, photo researcher/photo editor

**Photo Credits**
Digital Vision, 1, 15 (Venus)
Getty Images Inc./Taxi/Lester Lefkowitz, 20–21; Taxi/Paul and Lindamarie Ambrose, 12–13
NASA/JPL, 15 (Jupiter); JPL/Caltech, 15 (Uranus); SOHO, 9
Photodisc, 11, 14 (Neptune), 15 (Earth, Mars, Mecury, Saturn, Sun)
Photo Researchers, Inc./Jerry Lodriguss, 7
SOHO (ESA & NASA), cover
SuperStock/age fotostock, 19
Visuals Unlimited/Adam Jones, 4–5

# Note to Parents and Teachers

The Exploring the Galaxy set supports national science standards related to earth science. This book
describes and illustrates the Sun. The photographs support early readers in understanding the text.
The repetition of words and phrases helps early readers learn new words. This book also introduces
early readers to subject-specific vocabulary words, which are defined in the Glossary section. Early readers
may need assistance to read some words and to use the Table of Contents, Glossary, Read More, Internet Sites,
and Index sections of the book.

Printed in China
5888/5889/5890    082010

# Table of Contents

# The Sun

The Sun is easy to find.

It is the brightest object

in Earth's sky.

The Sun is too bright

to look at.

Photos from space

give a clear view

of the Sun.

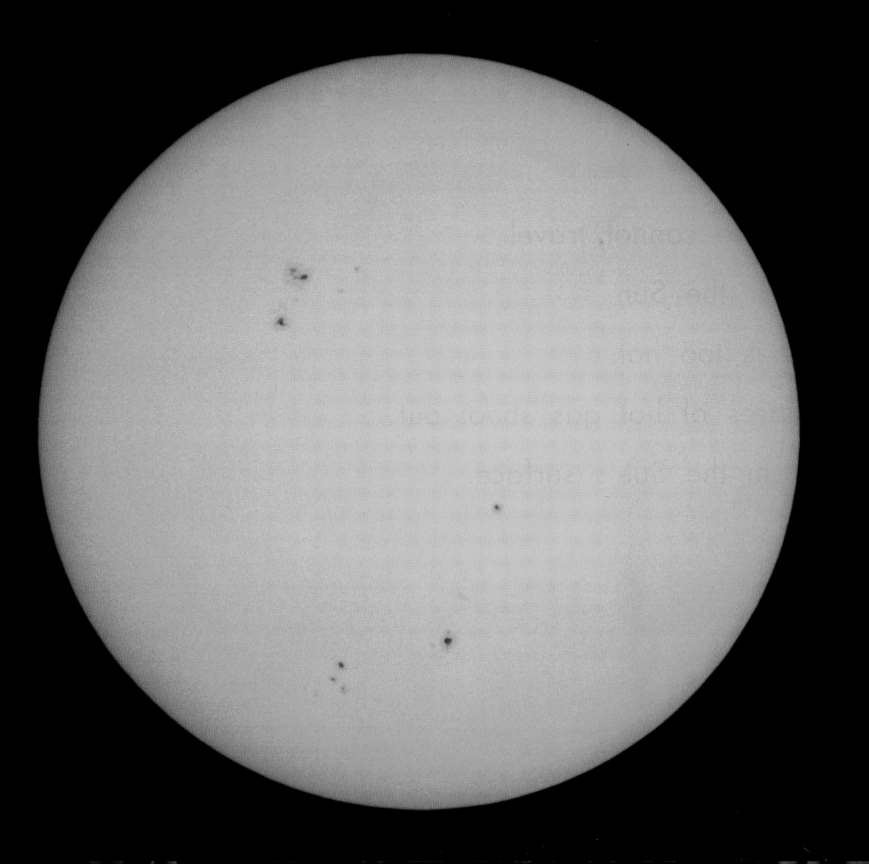

People cannot travel

near the Sun.

It is too hot.

Flares of hot gas shoot out

from the Sun's surface.

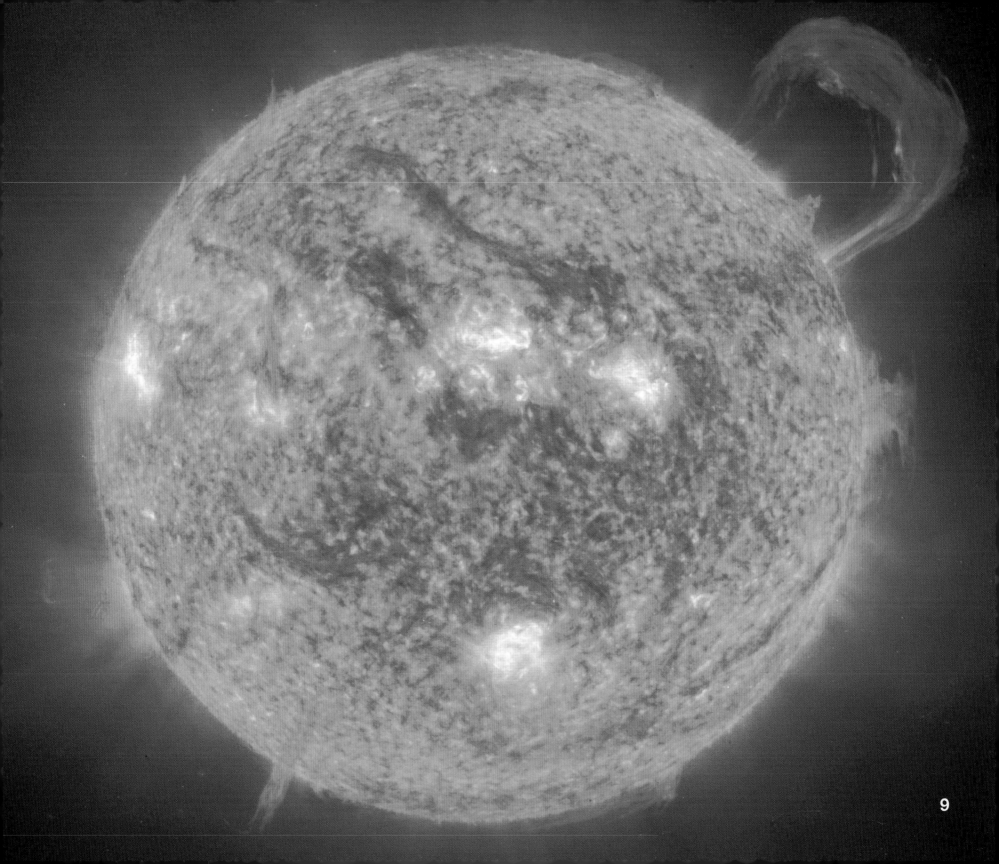

9

# A Star

The Sun is a star.

Like other stars,

the Sun is a ball

of burning gases.

It has no solid surface.

The Sun is one
of many stars.
It looks so bright
because it is the
closest star to Earth.

# The Sun in Space

The Sun is the center
of the solar system.
Earth and seven other planets
move around the Sun.

# The Solar System

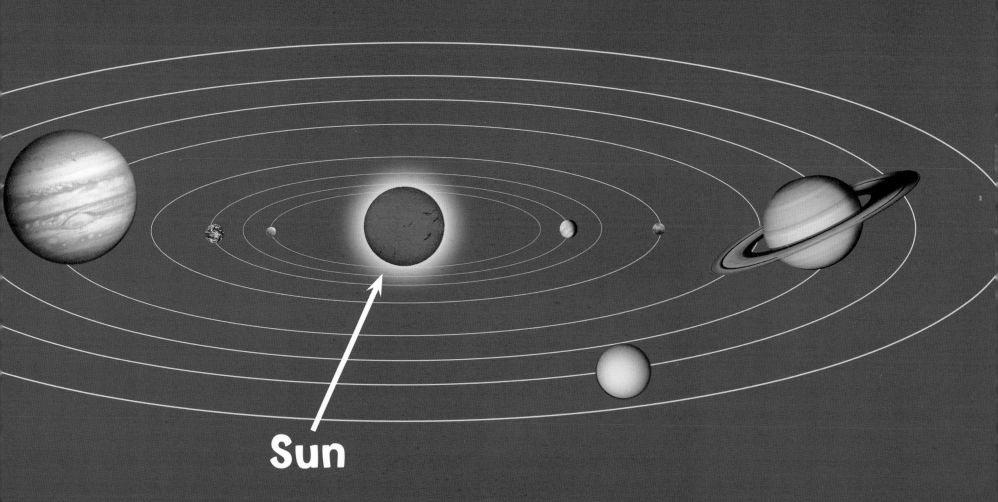

Sun

The Sun is much bigger
than the planets.
If the Sun were
the size of a beach ball,
Earth would be
as small as a pebble.

Earth

# The Sun and Earth

The Sun gives Earth

light and heat.

Plants need sunlight

to grow.

On Earth, the Sun

rises in the morning.

It sets at night.

You can use the Sun

to tell the time of day.

# Glossary

**Earth**—the planet we live on

**flare**—gas that shoots out from the Sun's surface

**gas**—a substance that spreads to fill any space that holds it; the Sun is made of hydrogen and helium gases kept together by gravity.

**planet**—a large object that moves around the Sun

**rise**—to move above the horizon; the Sun rises in the east every morning.

**set**—to go below the horizon; the Sun sets in the west every evening.

**solar system**—the Sun and the objects that move around it; our solar system has eight planets, dwarf planets including Pluto, and many moons, asteroids, and comets.

**star**—a large ball of burning gases in space

**surface**—the outside or outermost area of something

# Read More

**Bailey, Jacqui.** *Sun Up, Sun Down: The Story of Day and Night.* Science Works. Minneapolis: Picture Window Books, 2004.

**Eckart, Edana.** *Watching the Sun.* Watching Nature. New York: Children's Press, 2004.

**Rustad, Martha E. H.** *The Sun.* Out in Space. Mankato, Minn.: Capstone Press, 2002.

# Internet Sites

FactHound offers a safe, fun way to find Internet sites related to this book. All of the sites on FactHound have been researched by our staff.

Here's how:

1. Visit *www.facthound.com*

2. Choose your grade level.

3. Type in the book ID **0736867570** for age-appropriate sites. You may also browse subjects by clicking on letters, or by clicking on pictures and words.

4. Click on the **Fetch It** button.

**FactHound will fetch the best sites for you!**

# Index

Word Count: 171
Grade: 1
Early-Intervention Level: 15